To Jessica!

Enjoy the Dog Pals saving the world!

Best Wishes!

Copyright © 2021 Rob Kortus

All rights reserved.

ISBN 10 digit: 0-57-882460-4
ISBN 13 digit: 978-0-578-82460-4
Library of Congress Control Number: 2020916828

www.whendogpalsfly.com

When Dog Pals Fly across Point Nemo

Rob Kortus

A gift for:

Jessica

From:

Rob, Sophie, Sulley, & Wallace

Date:

April 26, 2021

Sophie, Sulley, and Wallace, I wrote this book for you three adorable and loving canines. Each one of your wonderful and cute personalities are revealed in your book and I'm sure everyone who opens this book will fall in love with the truly interesting characters that you are!

Friendship, my faithful canine companions, for loyalty is telling your best friend what they don't want to hear. Thank you for this reminder every day of my life.

On a very personal note, even after peeing and pooping in the house (occasionally), I still love you unconditionally. I'm not sure what life would be like without the three of you in my life.

I love you Sophie, Sulley, and Wallace.

WALLACE

Co-pilot, cute, whereas Sophie leaps before she thinks, and Sulley thinks five times before being forced to leap, Wallace never even thinks to think. The biggest heart of gold, very friendly, easily excitable and is simply the hilarious goof-ball in the pack.

SULLEY

Flight engineer, handsome, over thinker, over analyzer, over planner, lover of to do lists, and loves researching little-known facts. The voice of reason, or at least of caution.

Did You Know?
Sophie, Sulley and Wallace are the author's real life canine companions and are registered therapy dogs with Invisible Paw Prints, Inc.

Our story begins at the dog pal's helicopter tour business: Fly Dogs. A multi-level tree house in the biggest tree of the jungle, complete with pulleys, ladders and a tire swing.
The top level boasts a helicopter landing pad.

From inside the treehouse you hear Sulley clear his throat and he begins to sing happy birthday to a sleeping and snoring Sophie.

Tip!
Keep an eye out for hidden letters on some of the pages to uncover a secret message at the end of the book!

"Happy birthday to you, happy bir…"

All of a sudden, Sophie awakens! Slightly disoriented, she mutters: "Wha-?"

Sulley continues to sing. "Happy birthday to you…"

Sophie quickly interrupts with "AHHH!"

"AHHH!" Sulley responds.

Sophie yelps, "I hate that song!"

Sulley takes a step backwards. "I'M SORRY! I WAS TRYING TO START YOUR BIRTHDAY OFF WITH THE BIRTHDAY SONG!"

Sophie yells, "NO NO NO!"

Sulley asks whether Sophie really dislikes the birthday song.

Sophie replies, "YES I DO, ever since second grade! Don't you remember, Sulley?"

FLASHBACK to second grade! A young Sophie, Sulley and Wallace are present along with a young honeybadger called Rottilus, a harpy eagle, meerkat, quokka, aardwolf, chinese water deer, otter and fennec fox.

The entire class is singing happy birthday to Sophie over and over.
For some reason, Rottilus doesn't seem happy.
Sophie raises her arms in the air and shouts, "PLEASE STOP! THAT'S THE 77th TIME YOU HAVE SUNG THE BIRTHDAY SONG TODAY!

FLASH FORWARD

"Oh, yeah. I remember now. That was bad," says Sulley.

"My ears rang for a week," replies Sophie.

"Well then, what would you like to do today on your birthday to celebrate?" Asks Sulley.

Sophie stands proud and says, "let's do something cool and adventurous but DON'T sing happy birthday to me again!"

Sophie pauses and then shouts, "WAIT A SECOND! Where's Wallace?" "He's not still sleeping?" Says Sulley.

Suddenly, the chuf-chuf-chuf sound of the helicopter rotor blades echoes throughout the treehouse and jungle.

Sophie and Sulley rush outside to the deck!
There, they see crazy Wallace flying wildly through the jungle canopy.
They hear the whirring blades, and whining engine sounds.
The helicopter ricochets from tree to tree until a final palm tree sling-shots Wallace to a skidding halt in front of Sophie and Sulley!
Sulley sighs before calmy muttering, "Found him."

Wallace pops his head out of the cockpit and shouts up to Sophie and Sulley, "Happy birthday Sophie! I got you a surprise birthday cake!"

"Well, it certainly was a surprise, Wallace," asserts Sulley.

Wallace eats some frosting from his face and says, "Yum, you want some?"

Sophie tells goof-ball Wallace no and to clean up the helicopter and fly it back onto the helipad.

Setting out to celebrate Sophie's birthday, the Fly Dogs are in their crew positions and begin the take off sequence. Sophie operates the flight controls while Sulley scans all the instruments to ensure systems are operating normally.

Wallace finds some cake stuck to his navigational map, so he swipes it off with his paw and eats it.
"LET SOPHIE'S EXCITING BIRTHDAY COMMENCE!" Exclaims Sulley.
Sophie glances at Sulley with a smile.

"Let's go hiking at the state park," declares Sophie.
"Ooh! Exciting!" says Wallace.
The dog pals run up excitedly before screeching to a stop in front of the closed state park gate. All three dog pals state, "WHA??? "That's weird, They are NEVER closed this time of day."

"No problem! Let's go play laser tag," shouts Sophie.
"Ooh! Exciting!" says Wallace.
The dog pals run up and screech to a stop in front of the closed laser tag entrance.
"That's weird, they are NEVER closed at this hour."
Sophie looks disappointed and says, "Well, I'm thirsty! Let's go to my favorite juice stand." The dog pals depart.

"Here are your drinks," says the suspicious looking employee. "The cups are made from the orange peels."
"What did you just put in there?" asks Sophie.
"Peanut butter cup pieces!" replies the employee.
Sophie takes a big gulp of juice and all of a sudden, her voice changes. She can't control it! *"Testing, testing, one two three."* Sophie grabs her throat in total surprise! Wallace gazes at Sophie and says, "What was that, Sophie?"
"That wasn't me" replies Sophie. Then, in a super weird voice again, she says:
"Testing, one, two, three. YES! MY PLAN IS WORKING! Mwahahaha!"
Sulley quickly says, "That voice sounds familiar."
They look around and the employee has vanished!
"We need help from the Great Grandma Memuzzer!" says Sulley, with a panic in his voice.

While flying overhead, the dog pals assess the landing area, land, and exit the helicopter. The three dog pals enter a mystical house. Out of a darkened hallway, they make out a shape moving towards them.
Wallace shouts, "Memuzzer! We need your help!"
"Greetings Sophie, Sulley, and Wallace. I knew you would come," says Memuzzer. All three dog pals give Memuzzer a big hug! Memuzzer begins singing, "HAAAPPY--"
"NO MEMUZZER!" shouts Sulley!
"THE WORLD IS MINE! MAHAHAHA!" Sophie shouts in the weird voice again. Memuzzer stops singing and gazes at Sophie quizzically. She murmurs softly, "Well, that's interesting."
"*THAT'S* what we need your help with," says a concerned Sulley.
"Sounds like a voice-control spell," says Memuzzer. "Here!" she says while handing Sophie a mysterious looking box. Sophie opens it to find a glowing object.

"Whoa! Cool! What is it?" asks Wallace.
"You don't know?" replies Memuzzer.
Sulley inspects the object that Sophie holds in her hands.
Sulley says, "It's a bismuth crystal."
"Yes!" says Memuzzer.
"But what does it do?" asks Wallace.
"It is a secret crystal with powers," says Memuzzer.
The weird voice emerges from Sophie again: "I must contact my army and enact my plan!"
Wallace quickly says, "Does anyone else think that voice sounds familiar?"
Searching for an answer, the dog pals look to Memuzzer.
Memuzzer looks back and says, "Oh! You thought I'd know how to reverse the spell and return Sophie's voice to normal? Nope. Sorry. But I have heard of this spell before, in myth. The spell must be broken."
"What else do we need to know, Memuzzer?" asks Sophie.

Memuzzer blows dust from an ancient book and opens it.

"It sounds like someone has found the recipe for vocal control, contained in the Voynich manuscript. You must go to where that person is, stop them, and retrieve the Voynich manuscript. You must find out how to use the bismuth crystal to reveal the secret lair. Sulley, you must use your nose and your search and rescue skills to locate the entrance to Rottilus' secret lair.

Wallace inquires, "But where do we go?"

Sophie begins to pant heavily as if she was climbing a mountain. The weird voice says, "Almost back to my secret lair!"

Memuzzer replies, "My educated guess is that you need to go to Point Nemo."

Sophie's weird voice once again: "Wheeee! Now I'm sliding down into my secret cave!"

"What cave?" says Wallace.

Sophie lowers her head and says, "Aww. I wanted to have a fun birthday, not chase after a megalomaniacal evil mastermind, intent on world domination!"

The weird voice once again starts, "Happy Birthday to me, happy bir--"

Sulley places his hand over Sophie's mouth to silence the weird voice. Memuzzer says, "This is much worse than I thought, you must hurry to Point Nemo. Point Nemo is an area in the ocean farthest from any land in the world. Astronauts would probably be closest to that point. There is no land, just water. When you get there, you must use the bismuth crystal to find Rottilus' secret lair. Sophie, here is a birthday present from me."

"What is it?" says Sophie.

"It is an Egyptian Amulet found by a 12 year-old girl. It is known to protect you from evil and danger," exclaims Memuzzer.

"THANK YOU Grandma Memuzzer!" says Sophie.

"As per my GPS reading, we have arrived at Point Nemo." says Sulley.
"I don't see anything," says Wallace.
Sophie replies, "Remember what Grandma Memuzzer said; start playing around with the bismuth crystal. We must hold it in the sunlight at the correct angle and speak the code words to reveal Rottilus' secret lair."
"What were the code words?" asks Wallace.

Sulley holds the bismuth crystal in the air, twisting and turning it in the sunlight. "Skizzle, skuzzle, shebadoobie!" he says.
The bismuth crystal catches the light and a massive volcano ascends from the ocean!

Landing checklist complete," says Sulley.
"Roger," replies Sophie. "This is going to be a tough landing on this volcano slope."
"Whoa! Great landing!" says Wallace.
Sophie replies, "Thank you!" Then all of a sudden, Sophie's weird voice says "Ooohhh, rubby dubby! I'm singing in the tubby!"
Sulley and Wallace begin to laugh uncontrollably at Sophie.

The dog pals climb out of the helicopter near the top of the volcano. Sulley raises his nose and air-scents. "I smell something earthy and moldy."
"Yum! Wet mold!" says Wallace.
Sophie and Sulley stare strangely at Wallace.
"What? I haven't had lunch and I'm not feeling very picky right now!" says Wallace.
"There! The entrance to Rottilus' secret lair!" exclaims Sulley.
"Good job," says Sophie.

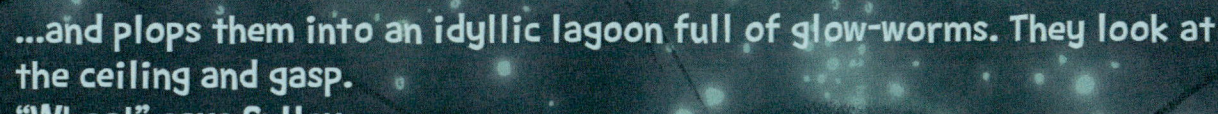

...and plops them into an idyllic lagoon full of glow-worms. They look at the ceiling and gasp.
"Whoa!" says Sulley.
"This is the prettiest evil lair I've ever seen," replies Sophie.
"Look Sophie! A birthday cake!" shouts Wallace.
Sophie replies, "Hmm... That's strange. Hey! I can't move my legs!"

"Can you move your legs?"
Sulley and Wallace reply simultaneously, "Nooo! I can't move my legs, I am stuck! Can't move a paw!"
All of a sudden a weird voice echoes throughout the cavern. "MWAHAHAHA!"
"That voice sounds familiar..." says Sophie.
"It's the same voice that has been coming from Sophie's mouth!" says Sulley as the fly dogs exchange looks.
Then, Rottilus steps out in his battle armor and strolls into the cavern.
"Rottilus?! From second grade?!" says Sophie.
"So, you remember me." says Rottilus. He then strolls by his birthday cake, swipes his finger through the frosting and eats it.

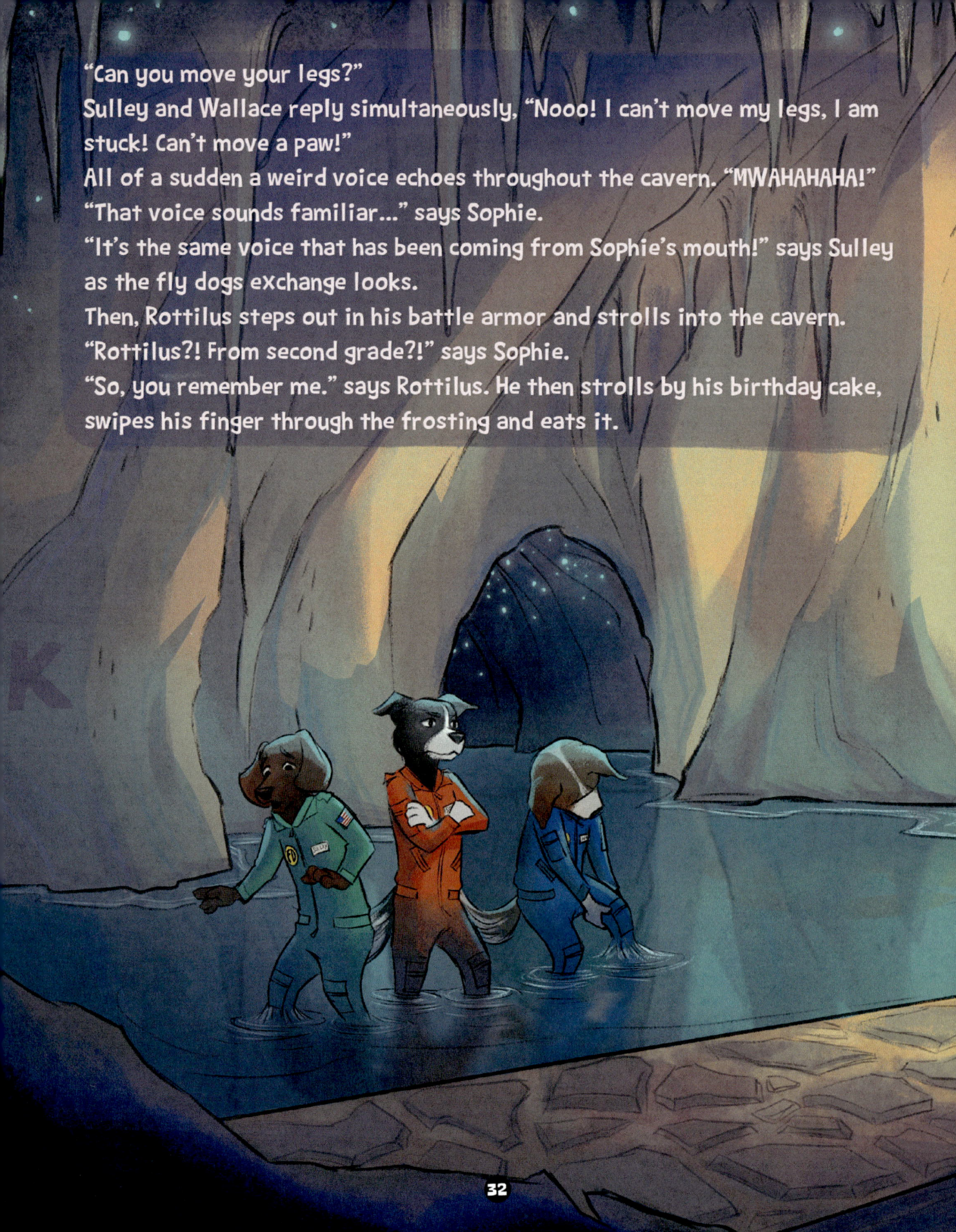

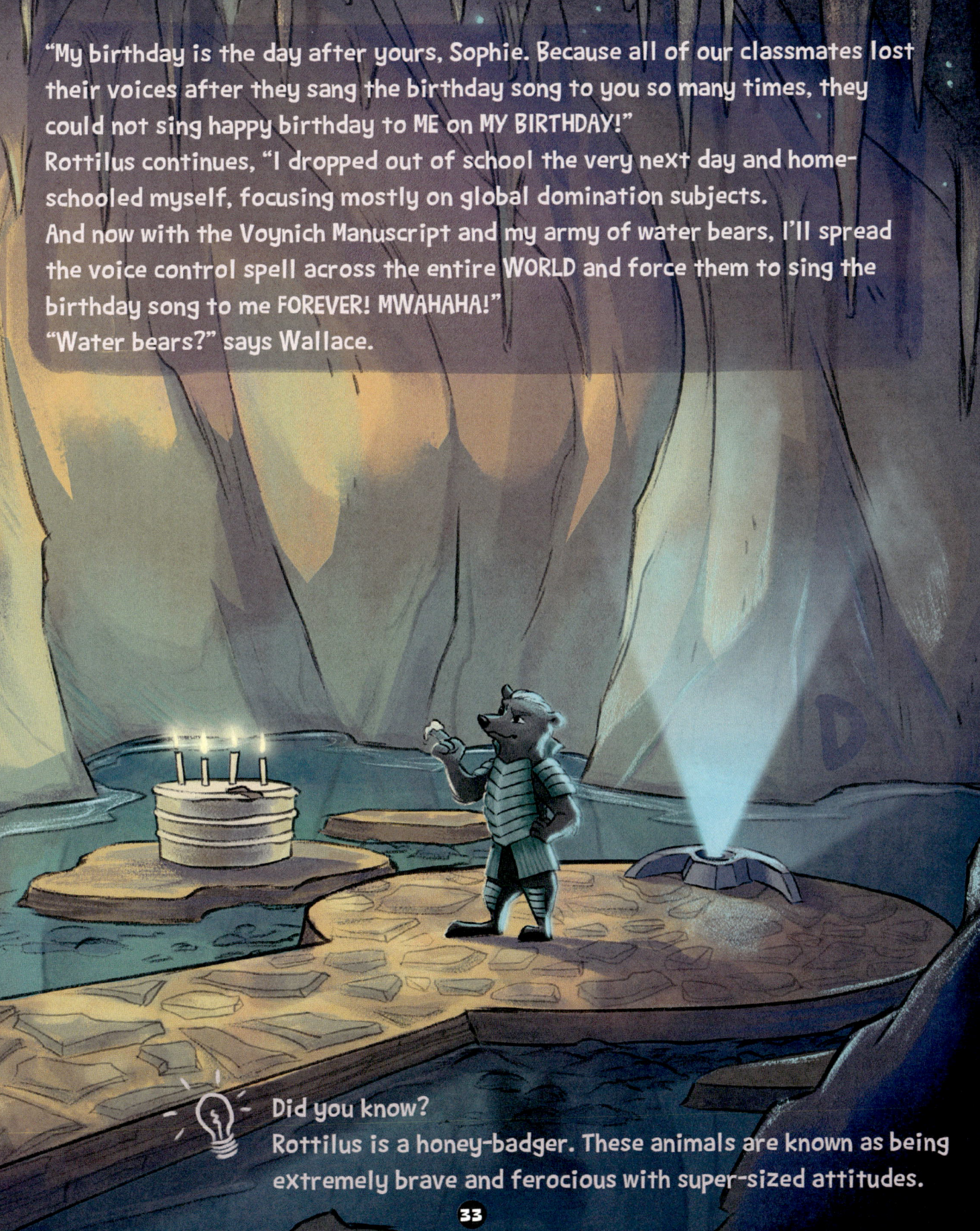

"My birthday is the day after yours, Sophie. Because all of our classmates lost their voices after they sang the birthday song to you so many times, they could not sing happy birthday to ME on MY BIRTHDAY!"

Rottilus continues, "I dropped out of school the very next day and home-schooled myself, focusing mostly on global domination subjects.

And now with the Voynich Manuscript and my army of water bears, I'll spread the voice control spell across the entire WORLD and force them to sing the birthday song to me FOREVER! MWAHAHA!"

"Water bears?" says Wallace.

Did you know?
Rottilus is a honey-badger. These animals are known as being extremely brave and ferocious with super-sized attitudes.

Wallace replies "Will the water bears play fetch?"
"Silence!" commands Rottilus. "Water bears can withstand temperatures as cold as minus 328 degrees, and as hot as over 300 degrees Fahrenheit. They can also withstand radiation, boiling water, up to six times the pressure of the deepest ocean depths and can even survive days in the earth's low orbit! So, they are the perfect army to help me conquer the world. They also never ask for anything, which is great because I'm very selfish!"

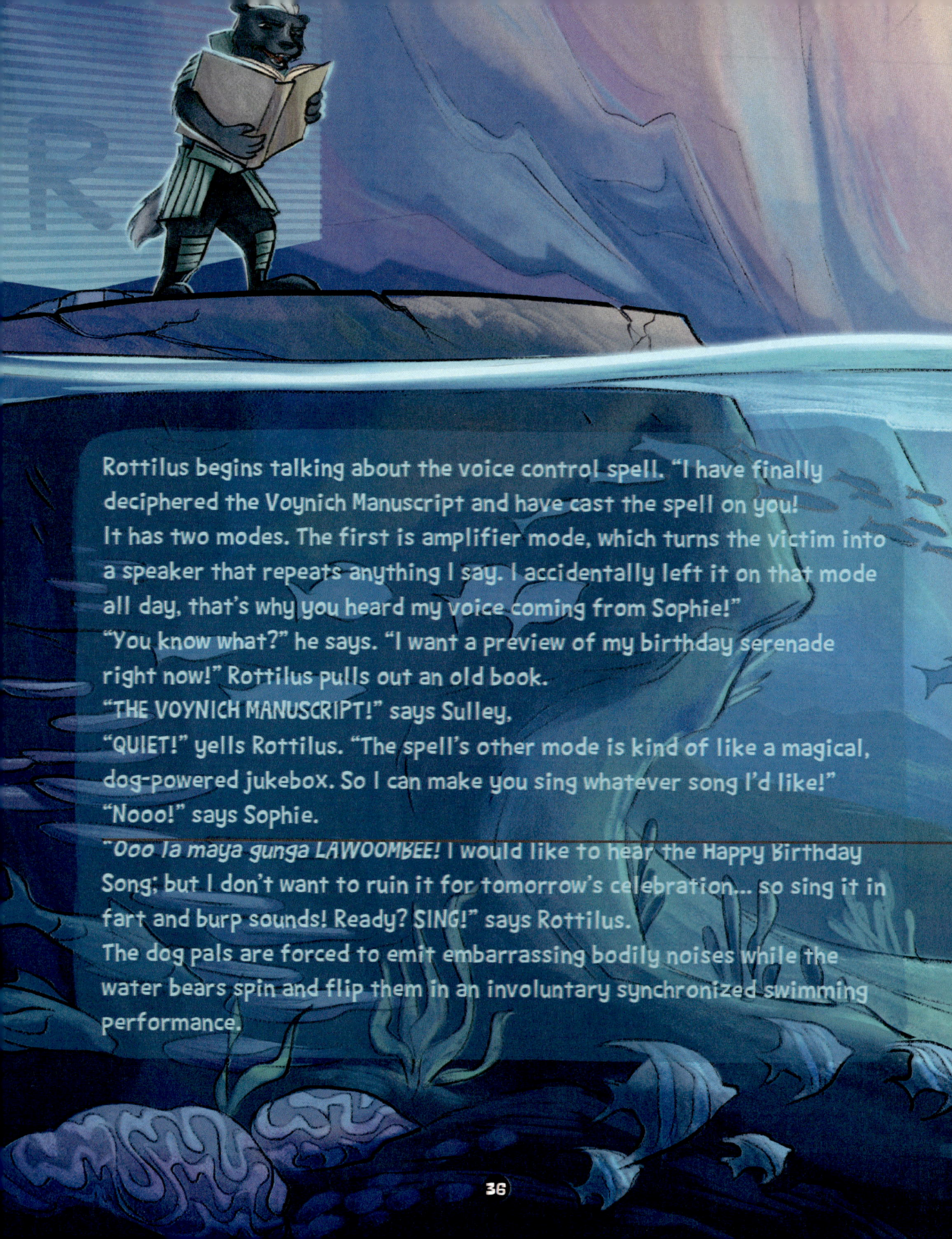

Rottilus begins talking about the voice control spell. "I have finally deciphered the Voynich Manuscript and have cast the spell on you! It has two modes. The first is amplifier mode, which turns the victim into a speaker that repeats anything I say. I accidentally left it on that mode all day, that's why you heard my voice coming from Sophie!"

"You know what?" he says. "I want a preview of my birthday serenade right now!" Rottilus pulls out an old book.

"THE VOYNICH MANUSCRIPT!" says Sulley,

"QUIET!" yells Rottilus. "The spell's other mode is kind of like a magical, dog-powered jukebox. So I can make you sing whatever song I'd like!"

"Nooo!" says Sophie.

"*Ooo la maya gunga LAWOOMBEE!* I would like to hear the Happy Birthday Song; but I don't want to ruin it for tomorrow's celebration... so sing it in fart and burp sounds! Ready? SING!" says Rottilus.

The dog pals are forced to emit embarrassing bodily noises while the water bears spin and flip them in an involuntary synchronized swimming performance.

Rottilus laughs and says "That was brilliant!" He claps his hands in applause. "Now, I've got some unfinished business to attend to. I will be back soon! Water bears! Do not let them escape!" commands Rottilus.

The water bear leader on the hologram replies "Sir, yes sir!"

Rotillus and the Japanese spider crab exit.

Wallace says, "What are we going to do?"

Sophie says, "Water bears, let us go please!"

"No way! We cannot release you." says the water bear leader. "But that is very nice of you to say please. Rottilus has never said please to us."

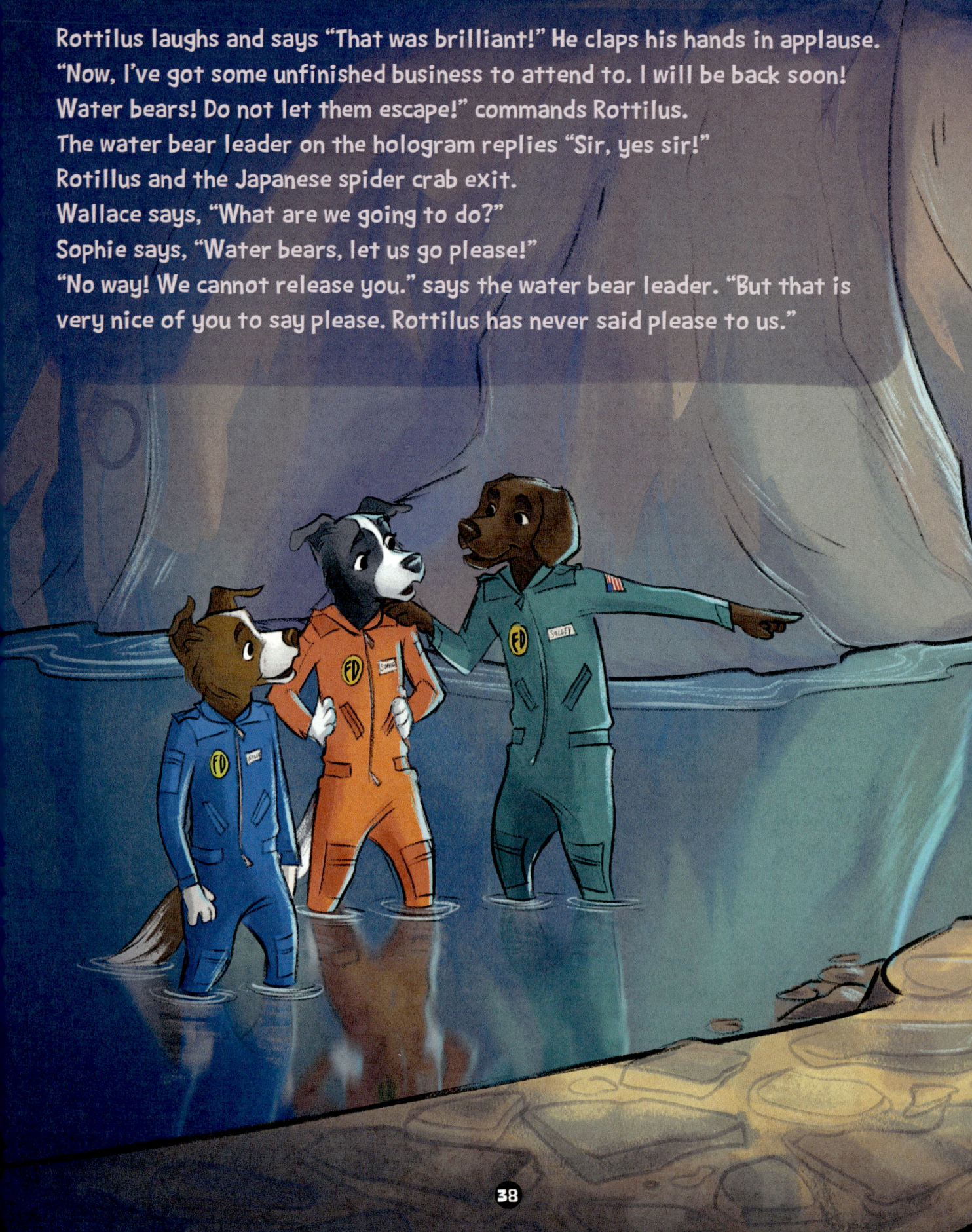

Wallace replies, "What if we say pretty please with sugar and whatever water bears find delicious on top?"

"We extract the fluids of animals and plants with our sharp, piercing mouths. So basically, we find you delicious!" says the water bear leader.

Wallace quickly replies, "Oh! Then I take that back! I thought you were going to say you liked birthday cake frosting or something."

"We wouldn't know. We've never had a birthday cake or a birthday party. Rottilus has never allowed us to have one... And today is five million of our birthdays."

Sulley says, "Sophie, Wallace!" He points at the birthday cake.

"Really?" says Sophie.
"Well, happy birthday water bears!" says Sulley.
The water bear leader wipes away a tear. "Rottilus has never allowed us to celebrate our birthday."
Sophie swallows hard, takes a deep breath and forces herself to start singing. "Haaaappy..." Wallace and Sulley join in. "...birthday to you! Happy birthday to you! Happy birthday dear water bear army! Happy birthday to you!"
"Wow Sophie! You hate thay song." says Wallace.
"Yeah, but they needed to hear it." says Sophie.

"Here." Sophie pulls out her birthday gift from Grandma Memuzzer, the Egyptian amulet and gives it to the water bears.

"For us? Are you serious?! Our first ever birthday present!" says the water bear leader. All of the water bears stare at the gift in awe.

"What is it?" asks the leader.

"It is an Egyptian amulet. This one is 3,200 years old." says Sophie. "It is a good luck charm. It's supposed to protect you from trouble."

All of a sudden, millions of water bears start saying, "THANK YOU! THANK YOU!" Over and over again.

"You are very welcome, all of you!" says Sophie.

"THANK YOU, THANK YOU!" The thank you's continue...

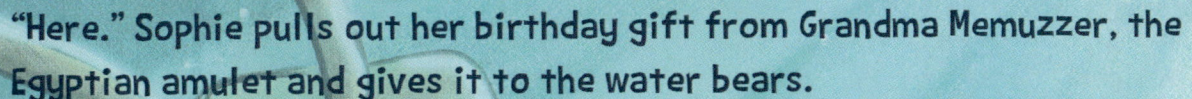

"That does it! Let's free them of this voice control spell!" shouts the water bear leader. "We remember Rottilus reciting this several days ago. Water bear army, recite the magical freeing spell with me!"
Millions of water bears begin to recite the spell to reverse the voice control! "Sheemee hoktoobee MYOCOKIE!"
"Again!" says the water bear leader. "Sheemee---"
Sophie begins to feel a cool, tingling sensation in her throat.
"I think the voice control spell is gone! THANK YOU, water bears!" says a gleeful Sophie.

The dog pals sneak into Rottilus' secret office where he goes through fantastical outfit after fantastical outfit in his walk-in closet. "None of these are grand enough!" says Rottilus. Sulley sneakily steals the Voynich manuscript from Rottilus' safe and hands it to Sophie. Wallace takes a wooden tablet from a safe behind a painting. Rottilus turns around and the dog pals jump out in front of him, surprising Rottilus!
"How did you get in here?!" says a confused Rottilus.

"Haha, how do you like this viral spell?" says Sophie. She cites a spell from the voynich manuscript. "Ooo la maya gunga LAWOOMBEE!"
Sulley and Wallace join in. "Ooo la maya gunga LAWOOMBEE!"
Sophie says "We'd like to request *The Song That Never Ends*... until it ends!"
Rottilus grabs his throat. "Noooo!!!" He starts to sing: "*This is the song that never ends...*"

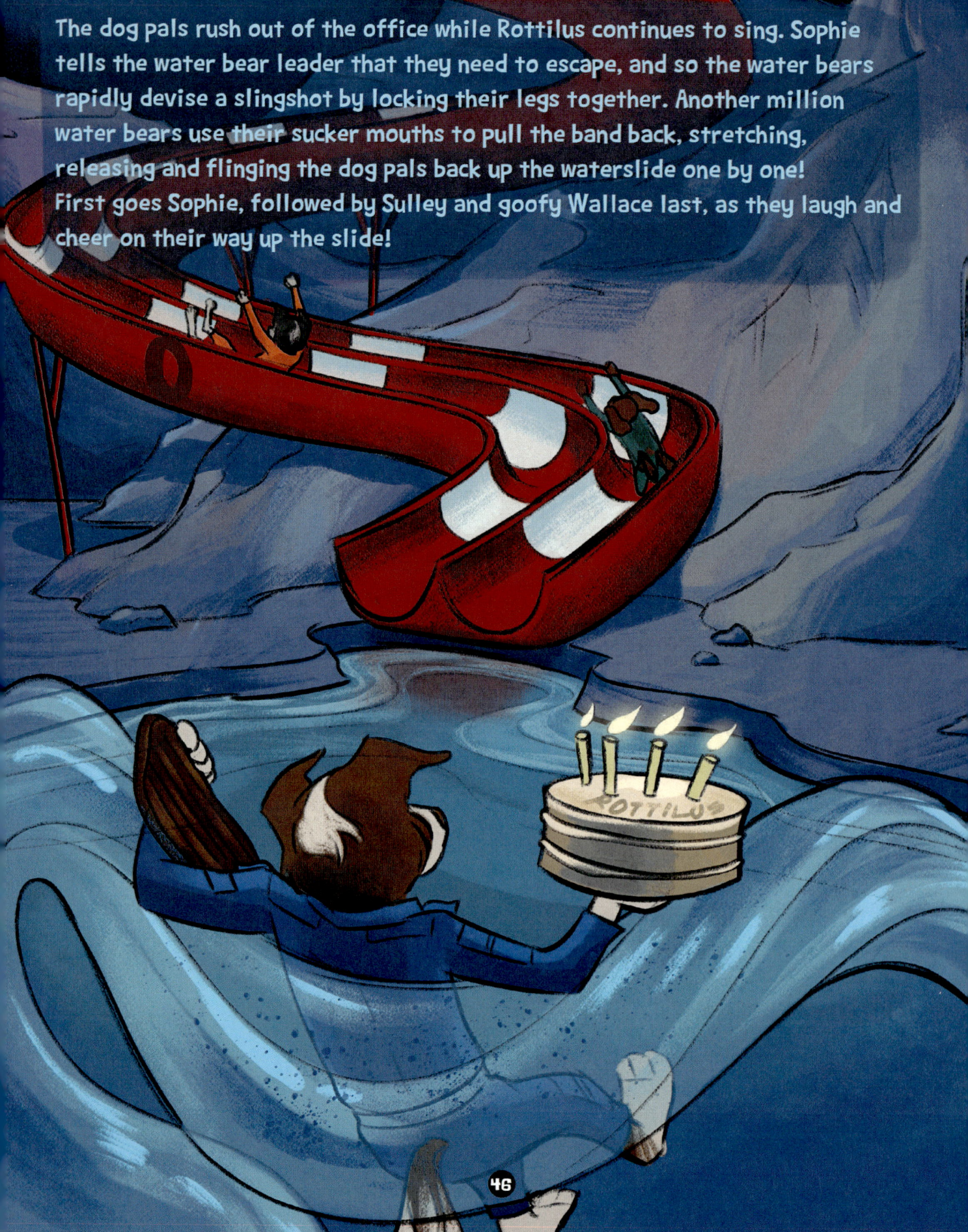

The dog pals rush out of the office while Rottilus continues to sing. Sophie tells the water bear leader that they need to escape, and so the water bears rapidly devise a slingshot by locking their legs together. Another million water bears use their sucker mouths to pull the band back, stretching, releasing and flinging the dog pals back up the waterslide one by one! First goes Sophie, followed by Sulley and goofy Wallace last, as they laugh and cheer on their way up the slide!

Rottilus comes sprinting out of his office lair after the dog pals and two million waterbears connect their legs together to form a tripwire. Rottilus' ankles strike the tripwire and he somersaults head over heels, landing on his butt! With his clenched fists in the air, he shouts in frustration: "I will find another army and be back to conquer the world, dog pals!"

The dog pals hop in the helicopter and Sulley asks Sophie to hover near the water's surface to blow water up and around the helicopter. The helicopter's rotors send hurricane-force winds downward, splashing the ocean spray up and around the Fly Dogs company helicopter.

A large water droplet lands on the windshield and Wallace holds the magnifying glass up for a closer look. He sees the waterbear leader waving goodbye.
All three dog pals shout "Bye water bears! Thank you! You're the best!" Then, Sulley flips the switch for the windshield wiper and with one swipe of the blade, the waterbears are sent back into the ocean.

The dog pals begin their long journey home. Once at the Fly Dogs jungle fort, Wallace pulls out the birthday cake with Rottilus' name on top. Wallace draws a line through Rottilus' name and writes Sophie's name in the frosting. He then lights the candles. "If we hurry," he says, "we might be able to do one exciting thing on Sophie's birthday wish list!"

Sophie replies, "Are you kidding?! That was the most exciting birthday ever! I'm exhausted. But do you know what I realized today? The best thing about birthdays isn't excitement or cake or NOT hearing the birthday song... It's spending it with my best friends!"

Wallace says, "how about one quick *happy birth---*"
Sophie interrupts and says, "Oh NO! Not again!"
Wallace replies, "What if we hum it?" All three dog pals laugh!
Finally, Sophie makes a silent birthday wish and blows out the candles.

Did You Know?

All throughout the book the objects and venues are real! Research this cool stuff on the internet!

Book Front Cover: Sophie, Sulley, and Wallace are the author's real-life canine companions! All three dogs were rescued! Wallace is a special needs canine. Wallace has epilepsy. All three dog pals are very healthy because they get lots of exercise!
Point Nemo is a real place out over the ocean! Nemo means "no one" in Latin. The treehouse is called Carolina Jewel (AKA treehouse castle). It was a DIY network build by the DIY Treehouse Guys! The author actually spent several days in the treehouse writing this book!"

Page 6-7: The helicopter is a cartoonish Coast Guard H60 Jayhawk which the author flew in his aviation career. The flight suit colors are the actual colors of the flight suits worn in the Coast Guard over past decades.

Page 12-13: All of these characters are real life animals: Honey badger, harpy eagle, meerkat, quokka, aardwolf, Chinese water deer, otter, and fennex fox.

Page 15: The poster on the bottom right is the first book in the series, When Dog Pals Fly Across America.

Page 19: There is the Carolina Jewel (treehouse castle) again!
We added in the helicopter landing pad!

Page 20: Hunting Island State Park is located in South Carolina. Area 53 Laser Tag is located in Brooklyn, NY. See the harpy eagle spying?

Page 21: Carlo Ratti's sustainable orange squeezer serves juice in bioplastic cups made from the peel! You have to check this out on YouTube!

Page 22: Grandma Memuzzer's house is actually an aerial view of Semery Mountain Palace at Ancient Siam (formerly known as Ancient City) near Bangkok, Thailand.

Page 23: Bismuth Crystal! You can actually make a bismuth crystal! It's a really cool process but you must have adult supervision! The material has to be heated so be extra cautious! These are so COOL!

Page 24: The Voynich Manuscript! It's pretty cool so research it! It's a 15th century codex – The world's most mysterious undeciphered manuscript! There is a great documentary on this book!

Page 28: Slope landing limitations for the Fly Dogs company helicopter is 15 degrees nose up or right or left wheel up and 6 degrees nose down.

Page 30: King Cobra water slide at Six Flags Great Adventure's Hurricane Harbor in New Jersey. Wow! Looks like a lot of fun!

Page 31: Glow worms in the caves in New Zealand. You have to YouTube search these creatures!

Page 32-33: The incredible Suytun Cenote is one of the best cenotes to visit on a day trip from Cancun. Awesome!

Page 34: Japanese spider crab called a Takaashigani (tall legs crab). These crabs are HUGE!

Page 35: The coolest creatures on earth! Make sure you read about these microscopic water bears or tardigrades! You won't believe what extreme survivalists they are!

Page 37: Yep! A red lipped batfish! How funny is that!

Page 41: This particular Egyptian amulet was found by a 12 year-old girl! She made the news!

Page 44: Wallace grabs the Rongorongo wooden tablet. Rongorongo is a system of glyphs discovered in the 19th century on Easter Island that appears to be writing or proto-writing. Numerous attempts to decipher have been unsuccessful. Just like the Voynich Manuscript!

Letter clues: Find the 38 hidden letters throughout the book, write them down on a piece of paper, and then cut each of them out, lay on a table and try to form a sentence.

Clue: One sentence with 10 words. Send your answer via the contact page at www.whendogpalsfly.com.

THANK YOU!

Rob Kortus writes amusing, action-packed and educational children's books; but for all ages! His characters are his real-life intelligent and funny canine companions who come across unique real-life objects and venues. Like the dog pals fly their helicopter, Rob is a retired Coast Guard helicopter pilot and academy trained Advanced Master Dog Educator and Trainer.

Rob and the dog pals share their home in Charlotte, NC and continue to make a lifetime of funny and loving memories. Their first book, "When Dog Pals Fly Across America" (Mom's Choice Award Winner) and this second book, "When Dog Pals Fly Across Point Nemo" are available on Amazon.com. Fun information on his blog and book signings can be found at whendogpalsfly.com.

"Bestowing kindness everyday will make your heart feel free!"

Special needs Dog Pal Wallace went to doggie heaven on January 27th, 2021. Rob, Sophie, and Sulley will miss you dearly and will love you forever our dear Wallace.

(A special thanks to Jessica Warrick, the brilliant illustrator for Rob's first book, "When Dog Pals Fly Across America" for her final touches on this amazing story! Many thanks from Rob and the Dog Pals!)

Made in the USA
Monee, IL
24 March 2021